Ink Smudged Dreams

- By the reading light

Debaleena Mukherjee

First Published in December 2020

ISBN: 978-93-5427-028-4

BLUEROSE PUBLISHERS

www.bluerosepublishers.com

info@bluerosepublishers.com

+91 8882 898 898

Cover Design:

Sanya Rastogi

Typographic Design:

Tanya Raj Upadhyay

Distributed by: BlueRose, Amazon, Flipkart, Shopclues

DEDICATION

To my husband - You give me the strength and confidence to be who I am; and you make me proud of myself. You give me hope.

To my daughter- You fulfil me and complete me. You make me feel that I am absolutely perfect as a person.

Both of you are my Life Force.

ACKNOWLEDGEMENTS

A book is much more than a manuscript. It is about the people in one's life. I have been very fortunate to have family and friends who have always opened windows of experiences and emotions for me.

My husband and my daughter:- For taking those book lists and patiently procuring books for me from your travels all over the world.
For calling me from bookstores, when on school trips, to ask- "Mama shall I get you a Romance by your favourite author?"

My parents who encouraged and supported my affinity for reading. As parents they never pushed me into career compulsions. What I chose, they appreciated. Every good composition that I wrote in class: they were proud of it. So I thank them for making this a way of life for me; rather than a struggle.

My teachers at school and university who knew me more than I'll ever know myself. They gave me the confidence to follow my dreams, however big or small. They taught me that life is not about water tight compartments. Everything, every day merges to emerge as another new day.

My friends who have praised, encouraged, cajoled, scolded, and almost sat on my head to make me write. They had faith in this friend.

My cousins who praised and exclaimed over my Facebook posts, and made me feel that I could write.

My little library at home. It's my window to the world. And those books are the spirits of life that fill my days.

To all the librarians I've met in my life. They led me to the right books at the right time. They took special interest, bent rules, spent extra time, and got me the books I wanted. They added their own too. I remember getting eight books for study material, instead of the allotted two, during my university days; because the librarian gave me his library card to use.

To the Publishing Team at Blue Rose for their support and guidance.

This I know that Someone up there is watching over me. My prayer and thanks to Him.

Thank You!

PREFACE

That day when I wrote my first poem: I took myself by surprise. And then came the realisation that I could not- not write this poem. I knew that I was where I am meant to be. But how? For I've always thought poetry writing is an artisan's craft. It is then that I knew that poetry is an outpouring, a sharing, a spiritual connect with yourself. I knew that I was talking to myself through those wobbly lines. When I read that poem later on; I felt I had put a bit of myself on paper.

There's always been a lot of writing that I've done, and I wrote volumes. I wrote as required. But my poem: I wrote myself into that poem. I wrote with all of me. My inhibitions, my quibbles; all vanished. This was an unapologetic acceptance of myself. I was happy with myself. That poem was my construction, my creation: my own little castle of words. It didn't matter if it was a sand castle. It was a wonder world of words and wordless emotions. That's why perhaps I could, to use a cliché, pour my heart out in these poems.

There is no self-consciousness in poetry. There is only self-awareness. When words become poetry, the "I" in the "Me" doesn't matter anymore. Only the world around me matters. And that is a very comfortable place to be in. Here, I found my freedom , my heart's ease.

My poems are my love letters to 'Life'. In this poetry, I surrender to all that is within me. I say what I feel, not what is expected. I write in a rhythm that's absolutely my own. I am in sync with my inside world. Most of all there is a sense of tranquil surrender. Perhaps that is why I had to wait all these years before I could write poetry. Was I being overconfident? No! Was I being arrogant? No! It is just that I was now very sure of what I needed.

This is a very roughly cobbled together collection of poems. I wrote them over a period of two years-anywhere, anytime: thanks to "e- legibility". Who says poetry and "qwerty" are not compatible!

It has been a very exhilarating and liberating journey for me. There are no wars, rebellions or proclamations in my poems. These are the doodles and scribbles of the smiles and tears of an unexceptional woman. I sit in my little library every night and drowse with these ink- smudged dreams : blurred yet glowing by the reading light.

Debaleena Mukherjee

CONTENTS

I. HYMN TO THE EARTH

1.THE EARTH WILL SING AGAIN

The Earth will sing again;
And raptly we will listen.
The Earth will caress us again;
And miraculously we will heal.

Too much was taken, too little returned,
We stripped her down to nothing.
We scratched and ripped and clawed at her,
We tore her sinews and wrenched her spirit.

She bled, she wept
Vulnerable and in pain,
Then she hardened, closed off herself,
And burnt herself relentlessly in the sun.

The rocky harshness flung out our lives,
She refused to soak up our sins.
Her stony depths denied us succour,
She stopped softening to our pleas.

The Earth had given,
Given more than she had to give.
Her body was parched, her voice rasped,
She begged us for relief.

And then her wrath was aroused;
She now rose up enraged,
Her pain had become her power,
She screamed 'no more, no further than this'.

We wept and we sickened,
We fought the enemy that devoured;
We pleaded for her mercy
But she had none to give.

So we crept indoors and waited;
We waited desperately for her to heal.
But little did we know how long she'd rest
Before she could begin to heal.

2. THE COLOUR OF WATER

Do you know the colour of water?
I've seen its many hues.
In that little pond of weeds
It is moss, dull and yet lush green.
I walked to the little lost stream,
Where it flowed clear blue.

It rained all through the day
And the water poured silvery grey.
It rained throughput the dusk
In sheets of dreary grey.

It rained all night and the windows streamed
With opaque jets of black.
The water gushed in inky spurts
That had the darkness of the wind.

The rain came down, the seas frothed
With frenzied foams of white.
The rains came down and the rivers boiled
With the blackness of the night.

Those puddles of placid blue on the streets
Had turned to fierce whirlpools of white.
A stark white pallor of flood and fear
Churned the currents that rushed to devour.
Do you know the colour of water?

Yes, it is the colour of life.
In the homely urn it's clear,
In tsunami it is white.

It sucks and pales the blood of life to pink,
It sweeps life's debris in brown and blood.
In bliss it feeds the fields in green,
In anger it hurls the trees in black.

Water's peace is pure and blue,
Crystal bright; still and fresh.
Water's wrath is ruthless black,
Or the colourless hue of death.

So do not seek to colour water
With the pettiness of your mind.
With tints of yours and tints of mine,
Or shades of right and shades of wrong.

For water is the living spirit
That takes the colour of nature and life.
Water is that fluid changing power
That chooses its colours from the palette of Time.

3. SUMMER IN OUR LAND

Summer is here.

Summer is here in a riot of colours.
Summer is here in sullen splendour.
Summer is here in the toasted grass.
Summer is here in the sizzling boughs.

The sunburst of yellow in some brazen bushes.
The glorious crimson in some barbaric hedges.
The vivid violet in some drooping creepers.
All baked in the kiln of summer fire.

One tree is fecund with plump mangoes.
One tree is redolent of knobby jackfruits.
One tree is glowing with ruby litchis.
Laden are trees with fruits that cup the sunlight.

Summer is the cleansing fire for the shriveled winter dregs.
Summer is the explosion of flames after the chill and grey.
Summer is the whiplash across the sinews and the senses.
Summer is the forge for new strengths and new ways.

Summer is a punishment for the rages of the heart.
Summer is the promise of quenching a raving thirst.
Summer is the softness of twilight April showers.
Summer is a whim of sudden breezes and sultry, hot hours.

Summer is the cracked, smouldering earth,
Summer is arid with the baked clay and dirt.
Summer is a gasp filled with the heat and the dust,
Summer is the burgeoning pain before birth.

Summer is of scalding waters, and blinding sun.
Summer is of heady scents and cloying tongues.
Summer is of scorching heat and searing breezes.
Summer is of burning noon, and stifling sleep.

Summer is the womb for the ripe and the raw.
Summer is the urn for the plenty and the sparse.
Summer is long and summer is fierce.
Gorgeous and fiery is the summer in our land.

4. A DRIVE

One summer afternoon,
The long road ahead.
Shadows flee with the car,
While the horizon glints afar.

The clouds flit in the blue sky,
The heat haze blurs the distant hills.
The warm breeze ruffles the heat,
While the car and horizon speed to meet.

Flowers bloom by the wayside;
Tumbled bushes wild and unnamed.
Sun bursts of yellow and baubles red,
Nature sunburnt, wilted but never defeated.

The sunlight bounces off the windows,
The molten tar unrolls ahead.
The scorch and glare the rocks reflect
The arc of rays that the windscreen deflects.

In the sky the sun rays pierce the dust motes,
And a lone beam dazzles the blue chrome.
The car whizzes, the summer light overflows:
While I sit and give thanks, for all that heaven allows.

5. THAT LITTLE LANE

Did you see that little lane?
The one that trickled into the trees.
From the stern pitch, all tarred and plane,
It suddenly decided to set itself free.

I saw that little lane as it plunged into the fallen leaves.
With what pluck it hugged the trees,
And merrily spilled into the green.
Like a stream it wound through the roadside woods,
Through the pebbles, and over the moss.
Like a tattered ribbon it twined around the bushes in knots of golden dust.

Let us wander down that way!
We will follow the sun dappled path.
We will stroll and we will pause; as we chat about this and that.
We will watch the sun and shade, listen to the trill of birds.
We will pick some wayside flowers,
We will not wait for the world.

This little lane has hidden nooks;
Where we can for fairies look.
There are bushes and unknown plants;
Where we can stop to smell the flowers.

Yes, today we walked this lovely lane,
Today we stopped and touched the flowers.
These flowers have always bloomed for us,
They've bloomed by this wayside all these years.
But we were too busy with this world;
Too busy to pause and smell the flowers.

We will soon walk down this lane again,
We will stop, rest and then walk again.
We will take all the time we want;
We will take time to go down this lane again.

We will walk to the end of the road,
Even though it may not be the place we seek.
We are in no hurry today; we have no place to reach.
It may not be the place we seek; but it's the place we
were meant to be.

II. A PRAYER

1. PRAYER

Why do you plan a prayer?
Why do you list a prayer?
Why do you allot a prayer?
And why do you regulate a prayer?

For my prayer is the pulse of my being,
My prayer is the meaning of my words.
My prayer is the essence of my living,
My prayer is the sum of all my thoughts.

My prayer is the spirit of the world,
My prayer is the word both said and unsaid.
My prayer is a song with melody unknown,
My prayer is a journey to where my flesh cannot go.

So why do you plan a prayer?
Why do you set a time for that which is timeless?
Why do you list a prayer?
Why do wrap a frame around that which is formless?

Why do you allot a prayer?
Why do you bind that is which is infinite?
Why do you regulate a prayer?
Why do you give a name to the Name of all names?

For my prayer is a wish
That my heart needed but did not know.

2.THE DYER

I am just a tattered cloth
All coarse, drab and uneven.
I am just a strip of cloth
Of the roughest, humblest linen.

Oh Great Dyer pick me up
You are the Weaver and the Wheel.
Bleach me in that purest form
So that I could be, placed at Your feet.

Oh Divine Dyer dip me in your rainbow
Of the colours of both heaven and earth.
Cleanse me of all the pains and stains
And swirl me in your dyes of Love.

I am that humble strip of cloth
That tumbles in the dust.
I am that narrow strip of cloth
That is tossed near your dye filled vats.

Colour me oh Dyer with the hues of your will
Immerse me in those holy waters.
Dye me in the dyes of prayers
And plunge me in the urns of faith.

Then Oh Dyer draw me forth
Fresh and pure with dyes so deep.
That I can walk the paths of life
Wrapped in the cloth of humility.

The Divine Dyer is my Lord
He is the Painter and the paint.
The Divine Dyer is my Lord
My false colours He will erase.

3. EVENING STAR

When I looked to the evening sky Oh Lord!
Your evening star was there,
In the violet and pink- dusted sky
The evening star was blushing and pure.
The night deepened and then the star blossomed
From a blush to a glow.

In those childhood evenings Your star was yet to be a beacon.
For now it was a comfort, a presence that in my heart would grow.
As the days grew to tears,
Your Evening Star still rose in my winter skies.
From the shores of childhood to the shores of youth
It remained shining bright and high.

In the youthful golden dusk of orange tinted skies,
The Evening Star remained :
Blushing, gentle and shy.
The days grew longer, yet shadows lengthened,
The star blossomed from a blush to a glow.
In the evening of my youth, the Star
Was a hope: a promise for tomorrow.

Now, as the shores and ocean merge,
Your Evening Star still rises in the night.
All the shores end here where the sands of time

Mingle with the eternal waters and I stand and wait.
I wait to see that great light that shines in the horizon.
I wait for that mighty call to step into that timeless ocean.

The Evening Star still shines up there;
A lamp in the night that burns and twinkles.
In the gray and indigo dusk it glows: blushing and gentle.
Now the dusk grows into the night, and my day is done,
The star has already blossomed from a blush to a glow,
Its light tells me that this is life ,nothing lost nor won.

In that final hour of my lifetime,
Let Your Evening Star be my solace and my succour
.
Let it be the blessing for my days,
My only song and my only prayer.
Let Your Evening Star be with me
For time that was, time that is, and time that will be.

4. THE RIVER OF LIFE

There is the crowd on banks of River called Life:
The crowd that's here to jump in and swim.
There is the crowd on the banks of the River called Life,
To drink its waters and take a holy dip.

Let us go to the riverside to join that festival of Life.
We too will answer that great call,
And go with them to light the lamps of Life.

We will walk with that crowd and throng to the River called Life.
We will dive and plunge to the depths to bathe in the waters so deep.
We will cup that water in our palms and offer it to the skies,
Then with blessings from above, we will drink to the fill.

The crowd is calling, the bells are ringing,
The incense is in the air.
The chants are loud and heads are bowed
as hands are raised in prayer.

Today is the day my friend
When the crowd gathers by the riverside.

This is the moment my friend
When all celebrate Life by the River called Life.

I too will go to the riverside to join the festival of
Life
I too shall answer that great call,
And go with them to light the lamps of life.

III. THE GIRL

1. GLITTER GIRL

She walks the beaten track
But her head is in the clouds.
She walks the beaten track
But she looks at the stars.

She walks the beaten track
But she flits with the butterfly.
She walks the beaten track
But she shines like the firefly.

She walks the beaten track
But she floats on a rainbow.
She walks the beaten track
But her Unicorn is ready to go.

She walks the beaten track
But she sprinkles glitter on the mud.
She walks the beaten track
But her broom sweeps fairy dust.

She is you and she is me,
She is the shelter in the storm.
She is the anchor at the sea,
She is the port called home.

Her magic is ordinary,
Her magic is in each day's love.
Her magic is extraordinary
For she is all about love.

2. "GORI" GIRL

It's time we started working on your skin;
You are all of thirteen.
Start skin care right away
They all need you to be fair.

There are spices in the kitchen,
There is milk, and curd, and cream.
I will fix a mix and paste it on you;
Close your eyes, sit still; there's nothing for you to do.

You don't need to open your eyes,
You are not a part of this world.
You are bound by rules my girl:
You cannot scale the walls.

You have brains that swirl with thoughts,
You have skills that could take you far.
But what's the point of brains and strengths
When your complexion is not at all fair.

Floral creams and fruity lotions,
Slap and slather on your face.
It's the marriage mart my girl
That will decide your fate.

Fruits and veggies, juices and pulp;
You have to be a fruit salad, you have to apply what you cannot gulp.
So what if he's a fruitcake, or if he's a nut case,
He's after all the one who will look only at your face.

Ours is a land of dark blue clouds,
Ours is a land of dark, gold wheat.
Ours is a land of dark green ponds,
Ours is a land of dark clay fields.

Yet we look for Snow White's skins,
And we judge by fair and dark.
Yet we brand and label fresh faces,
And shop for foreign fairness creams.

3. BODY SHAME

Do not body shame me;
I am, after all a part of your body.
Do not body shame me
I grew in her womb.

Don't body shame me,
You planted the seed that became this "I".
Don't body shame me;
For yours is the chromosome Y.

There are generations of your genes
That have built, and shaped me.
Take a good look; there's a bit of your mother in me.
So better think twice before you body shame me.

You disapprove of my being,
You wanted the daughter you had imagined.
You are shocked that I am not
The human that you had in mind.

You had wished for a little doll,
With everything placed right.
You had thought of a wooden puppet
Whose strings you could jerk left and right.

But then I happened, and nothing seemed nice and right.

I was not the cute poster cut out,
For all I had were eyes and teeth,
Full of puppy fat and fight.

You were embarrassed if I was awkward,
You were cruel when I was hurt.
You were angry when I was gawky,
You blamed me for all the catcalls.

You barred me from dressing up, you said no to makeup.
You made me less than I was, you made me cover up.
You held me hostage for my genes; I paid ransom for your parts.
How did you forget that you made me as I was?

My strength came from myself,
My body learnt pride.
You body shamed me,
But didn't you really shame your own life?

4. SAY YES TO YOURSELF

Find your worth within,
Give yourself the nod.
Put your seal on all your thoughts,
Then say yes to yourself.

For what lies in that vastness out there,
Is a mad, mad maze.
If you start a journey on others' tracks
It will lead to nowhere.

All you will find is a mesh of alleys all wound up in one,
And if you cut across you may miss the turn.
If you take a detour; it is a blind lane.
You wanted the walk, then why did you break into a run?

Flag off your own life's tour,
Go book that ticket to living.
Pack your bag, set your life's clock,
Then say yes to yourself.

Take the step or the plunge.
In the midst of duty calls
Answer your own heart's call.
Then when the rains come, sail your paper boat of dreams.

Walk to where sky and earth meet,
For yours is this terrain rough and free,
Yours is this one life to live, and to feel.
If smiles start let them grow, and also let those tears flow.

Don't create a stranger called "You",
Give yourself the Permit.
Draw the map, find the route.
Then say yes to yourself.

5. MIRROR MIRROR ON THE WALL

I went in search of myself.
The self that they wanted to see.
I went in search of myself
Because they said I wasn't the right Me.

Yes, I made them my mirror,
My own mirror had said you're already "a wow girl".
But I made them my mirror,
They said that's not the ideal girl.

One flipped my hair to the left
The other changed my reds to pinks.
One disapproved what the other approved,
But I approved all that they said, as I wasn't allowed to think.

But my mirror never changed its mind;
It still said " that was the wow girl!"
I turned this way and that
And asked "how the wow girl?"

I tried other skins,
The mirror screamed "Oh please!"
I itched and chafed in alien skins,
But repeated "I have to please!"

Till the night I shed the skins
And stood naked before the glass.
The mirror exclaimed "look at this
The real you at last!"

I dusted and dug out myself;
The mirror polished me some more.
I turned this way and that,
The mirror shone some more.

My mirror never changed its mind:
It still said "that's my wow girl!"
I twirled and spun in my own skin:
Then smiled and said- "yes wow girl!"

IV. THE WOMAN

1. EVE MAKE YOUR EDEN

In the concrete jungle of my mind,
I dreamt of another Eden.
In the hollow tunnels of my heart,
I dreamt of another Eden.
In the barren fields of my life,
I dreamt of another Eden.

In this other Eden of my own
New, lush green thoughts would grow.
In this Eden of many new hues,
Secret hopes would bloom and grow.

I sat and wove so many dreams,
I wished and prayed for those new leaves;
Till one day I woke up and a voice said:
"Go out there and build the garden that you need."

Leave the four walls and pick up the spade,
Turn the dust and dig the clay.
Sink into the soul and tear the weeds.
Make the holy river feed your garden stream.

Dig with your despair, and sow with your hopes,
Drench with your tears, and plant with your vows.
Stand on that land and sprinkle with your smiles,
Protect with your wrath and nourish with your life.

Eden will blossom on this soil of your pain,
Eden will grow from the seeds of your mind.
Eden will flourish in the rains of your prayers,
Eden will sway to the breeze of your care.

The serpent will come, but it would have lost its sting:
For this Eve will not fall; she has found her wings.
The serpent will slither in, for your garden is wild and free.
It will wind itself, as it had before, round the Knowledge Tree.

There can be no more seduction with those secret hints of power,
You have tasted of the fruits with the strength of your endeavours.
The serpent will slide up and promise you the world,
But you are the new Eve, priestess of the Truth Tree.

In your Eden the gates are open, to all that is new.
Walls of hate are broken down, as the winds of change blow and storm.
Your Eden now is your sanctuary,
Your tranquil spirit and truth are its only keys.

In this Eden you will drink from the fountains;
Not of eternal life; but a life well lived and free.
In this Eden you will swing high and loudly sing
From the laden boughs of that Knowledge Tree.

Here no fruit is forbidden and you will eat your fill,
Of those apples that you boldly pluck off the tree.
So what if there's a treacherous serpent;
Serpents in paradise are meant to be.

For you are strong, you are the explorer in your own Eden.
You defied the rules to eat the fruit forbidden.
You bit into that luscious tempting orb
And set that core of wisdom free.

You ate the Apple's sweet flesh,
You then scattered the hidden seeds.
You savoured and then you shared,
The secrets of that Knowledge Tree.

Yours is the courage that broke the bonds,
Yours is the power to choose right from wrong.
You paid the bloodied price of freedom,
You wept in solitary pain ,but defeated demons.

For in the mysterious divine plan,
You were the blessed and the brave one .
Only you could dare to do, and bring to fruition
The promise of that Holy Wisdom.

Be Eve, dare to choose and fear not the strife.
Be Eve: free your spirit; and reach for love and life.

Be Eve: battle Evil, walk tall, and fear not the Fall.
Be Eve: embrace the Good; and rejoice in your Free Will .

2. THE WORLD WILL WAIT

Drink your coffee, sit down for a bit,
The world won't blame you.
Pause in your strides; breathe a little bit,
The world won't run away from you.

Don't lose touch with this world,
You know your emptiness is within you.
Don't fly from this world,
You know your demons are within you.

Hold on to each moment,
Time had never been hostile.
Caress every surface of your life,
The textures are yours to define.

Filter the toxic, do not try and dilute.
What is will be ; what is not- will not.
Find your space, find your solace;
For this is just the one life you've got.

Let go, unlearn,
Make your own mistakes.
Forget all those examples and comparisons,
Choose only what it takes.

What it takes to craft your own life,
Not a copy of someone else's tale.
Be yourself bold and firm, yes they'll gasp and plead.
Cut some bonds and break some ties, yes some will say they bleed.

Bend the bars, and break the glass,
Never mind if you topple over.
Better to breathe as you strive,
Not stifle behind those mind's prison bars.

3. WORLD WITHIN

Her world was big and sprawling,
Life happened all over that world.
Someone called, someone came, and someone asked.
She was the spoke, the rim and the hub,
She kept the wheels turning and often took the rub.

So many meetings, so many commitments.
So many niceties and so many assessments.
Of duty and pleasure; of gives and takes,
Of lists and promises; of how and when.

She moved with this flux,
She had entwined with the weave.
She shaped and spun,
Even as she blended in.

But there was another world;
A world of her very own.
A world within this other world,
That was still and calm;
With dreams and stories untold.

She sometimes stepped into her world and sat,
For here she didn't need to move.
Here she could be no one,
For here she had nothing to prove.

This was the world within herself;
A world that shimmered and changed.
A world that had no fixed rules,
A world where she never had to choose.

She built it with her inner thoughts,
She lived in it as the person she wished to be.
She shed all her social trappings,
And spun the magic as she pleased.

No this was not her hideout;
That's not what it was meant to be.
This was her inner domain,
Where her spirit roamed free.

This world was her stronghold
That strengthened her being.
This world was the power
That renewed her for living.

There is that world in each of us;
A little garden of thoughts and rest.
Little but oh so infinite,
Where no cost is counted, no dues to be paid.
No cautions given, no duties nor lists,
Just the magic of each new day.

4. SILVER LININGS

If the cloud had no silver lining
Do not blame the sky.
If the cloud has no silver lining
Do not use the rain to cry.

The sky has its own colours of sun and rain;
That swirl with all the hours.
The sky has its shifting winds and clouds;
That change with all the hours.

The sky just shelters and waits forever:
Its faith is in its waiting,
The sky just does what it's always done;
Its faith is in its serving.

Do not blame the sky for the clouds
That are grey, not glowing.
Do not chase the shooting stars
To find your silver lining.

I will use the silver in my hair,
That shines with all my years.
I will thread the silver in my hair
Through the leaden cloud of my fears.

I will weave the silver of my age
Into the empty rims of the clouds.
I will weave the silver of my life
Into the frayed edges of the clouds.

5. MY AUTUMN

I snuggle into the Autumn of my life,
It is my very own and precious time.
I sink into the Autumn of my life,
It is my time out of time.

In this Autumn of my life all is quiet and all is good,
Far into the night I sit and wait
And life and I speak in hushed tones.
I ask so many questions but find
that I don't need answers anymore.

Am I fulfilled? I don't really know.
Have I won the race? I don't really know.
But in this grey and mauve twilight tint
I know that I am content.

For in this season of fallow fields,
I know that all is quiet.
The years of frantic loss and win are done,
I am replete, I am quiescent.

My Autumn is a tranquil haven
For my weary spirit.
My Autumn is a fresh free space
For my soul to wait.
No, this is not about a journey's end:
This is the time I give me to myself.

Nothing asked, no demands;
I take it all, the way it is.
No regrets, no blame, nothing to complain.

In this Autumn I have found
That nothing was really lost.
It was all there in whole new forms
In ways that mattered most.

I snuggle into this Autumn of my days,
I have given my life in Someone up there's keeping.
Now I know that life is not made to measure
For life knows naught about tallying.

So here I rest, here I retreat:
Here in this autumnal space.
In this soft and gentle sun
There is heaven shining on my face.

6. LAMP ON THE PORCH

Life is there before you;
Fill it with a story that's only yours.
Life is all the alphabets,
Waiting for you write the story in your words.
There are so many roads for you to find,
There are so many curves and bends.
Follow the tracks or pave the way.
It's your terrain to mark or make.

But, if you choose to stay at home; to watch the distant roads,
That too is your power: a choice of your own.
No one said that all have to conquer,
No one said all have to discover,
You may choose to stand in welcome at your door.

You are the window to everyone's world,
You are the anchor and the port.
You are the "come home to", and "look back at"
For those that step across the threshold.

For what is a journey without the return?
What is the voyage without the compass?
What is the race without the point of start?
What is the win without the quiet rest?

Be the curtain that keeps out the dark,
Be the memory that guides the wanderer.
Be the lap that soothes the hurt,
Be the solace in the mad search.

You are the strength and the succour,
You are the hand that leads to the road.
You are the peace, and the pillar
For you hold the lamp and wait on the porch.

V. TEARS AND SMILES

1. LIVED?

Not lived life?
Yes you have.
Each moment you laughed or cried,
Every breath that you took and felt; you lived.

You thought the hour was empty;
Did you count the seconds you lived?
You thought the hour was unfinished;
Did you count each moment you fulfilled?

Did you see the winding roads,
Or did you only focus on the distant goal?
Did you stand at the crossroads to think,
Or did you walk only the high road?

Did you ponder at the signposts,
Or did you never make a choice?
Did you follow yesterday's tracks,
Or did you find a new path?

Did you wait at the tollgate,
Or did you venture into the uneven by-lane?
Did you follow the tail lights of the car in front,
Or did you turn off to find a different way?

Yes, you have lived.
Each minute of each day.
You have lived every day;
Not just the sum of all your days.

Turn the hourglass and watch the sand:
Not just to watch how fast the sand slips.
Turn the hourglass and watch the sand:
You'll see each grain is perfect; each grain is fulfilled.

2. REALISATION

I tried my best!
I gave of myself only for love.
I did what I had to do.
I did what I did; as I couldn't not do.

To each that I know
I gave what I owe, and more.
The dues of duty and of time,
With all of me, I gave of mine.

I clung too close; I held too close.
I looked up at, and looked to, too much.
I made them my world; and so I knew none of my own.
I yearned to be a bit of theirs, and then found myself alone.

There was no other way I could be,
For they made my world complete.
I left no space between them and me,
And never realised until it was too late.

That each life has its own breath,
Each name its own meaning.
Each one is another person,
Not all are bound to me.

So breathe first for yourself,
Cling first to yourself.
Give first to yourself
That love you owe yourself.

3. EMBRACE YOUR BOREDOM

Embrace your boredom
For it's your very own space.
Embrace your boredom
For it's your rare and special place.

In that void of nothing
Pour out all your thoughts,
In that hollow of waiting
Share all that's in your heart.

Fill your boredom with some dreams,
Chase away the blankness with some images.
Make some random, quirky sketches
With idle musings and absurd wishes.

Boredom is your very own canvas;
Fill it with the colours of your desires.
With brushstrokes of your choosing
Paint the landscape of your dreams and cares.

Embrace your boredom:
For it is a familiar feeling.
Give it some energy and some fun,
Pack in a punch of living.

The mind wanders in boredom
Down strange paths to stranger freedom.
In boredom nothing is forbidden, nothing barred,
Boredom is safe as it is never judged.

But boredom awakens the slumbering mind,
It unties the strings of duty.
It sets free the kites of imagination,
It gives the heart a holiday from reality.

So embrace you boredom,
It is that hour of just Being.
Of filling the soul with fresh new fields,
With green spaces of thinking, not just blank Doing.

4. IT HAPPENS

Life happens!
For once let me happen to Life.
Things happen!
For once let me take them as things, not everything.

Weaknesses happen!
For once let me make them my strengths.
Dreams break!
For once let me make a million dreams from those breaks.

Fractures happen!
For once let me use my crutches as tools.
Cuts happen!
For once let me flaunt those battle wounds.

Tears happen!
For once let me use them to cleanse.
Anger happens!
For once let me use it as a Rinse.

Life happened.
So I happened to Life.
The ordinary happened;
But I made it my one extraordinary Life.

5. UNKNOT ME.

I've tied my life in knots;
All twisted, gnarled and tortured knots.
The ropes there had been straight and smooth
But then I gripped them with my thoughts.

Knots of thoughts, then thoughts upon thoughts,
Biting knots, griping knots, panic knots and painful knots.
Always a slowly tightening fearsome knot.
Knots of my wishes and knots of my regrets for all that I had to do, but I could not.

I grappled with these knots of life,
They tore and broke the skin of my soul.
A noose of thoughts had me clenched
In a choking ,lethal stranglehold.

But the ropes long ago that had been so strong and smooth,
Were never meant for such knobbly knots.
The ropes long ago had been so strong and smooth,
Meant for bonds and ties of trust, not such tortured, heavy knots.

Let go of this death grip on that rope,

Let it sway and dance with hope.

Let the ropes be long and light,

Let them hold you safe and strong: and let your spirit freely fly.

6. ALL THE MEMORY LANES

When in the midst of a busy day,
A sudden longing catches you unawares.
A rush of memories, and forgotten moments
That fill your eyes with yesterday's bittersweet tears.

Fleeting flashes that pierce your heart
With long forgotten joys and hurts;
A glimpse of a face, the echo of a laugh,
The voices from a yesterday that you never forgot.

When in the rush, and to and fro, the clock stops and you pause.
The hands then rewind to hours of a day from long ago.
Some old voices whisper to you all those tales of old.
You softly smile at the faces from those days that are no more.

This is the place where Time takes rest,
This is the place where Life draws a deep breath.
This is the place where our spirits take wing,
This is the place where nothing ever ends, or ever begins.

For these are the moments only to be felt;
They flash and fade, they cannot be held.

They sharply pierce or softly search,
They do not shift with Time's fickle touch.

Memories are the remembrances of a life that was,
They are the 'Then' to the 'Now'.
They are the albums of thoughts from the past,
They are the "post its" from times now lost.

Memories can hug, and memories can hit,
Memories can search, and memories can heal.
They can renew or redress the wrong,
They can refresh and replay the song.

Yes!
My memories can find the blurred pictures
Of those days from long ago.
My memories can start the juke box
Of yesterday once more.

VI. OF LOVE

1. ASK OF LOVE?

What is love? The children asked?
What is love ? The youth asked?
What is love? The aged asked.
And yet here we are all waiting for an answer.

Love is you and I.
Love is they and us.
Love is All of us.

Love lingers in the corridors after the classroom closes.
Love waits at the bus stop after the bus leaves.
Love rustles in the diary after the rose has dried.

Love is in the wedding knots and the clothesline weighed with washing.
Love is in the sacred fire and the flickering gas stove.
Love is in the solemn ceremony and the morning sneezes.

Love is sandwiched in the shared burger at the store.
Love is in the clutched hands on the escalator.
Love is in the last piece left on the pizza platter.

Love is not logical.
Because love defies logic.

Love is exasperation,
Because Love whines.

Love is forgetful, but never forgets.
Love is curt, but not careless.
Love is bossy, but it is never the boss.

Love hurts , it always hurts.
Love wounds, love wounds again and again.
Love angers, love is angry.
But Love expects only Love in return.

Love. What is love?
We are all waiting for an answer.
We get no answer, but we always find Love!

2. PHONES

The candles were silky,
The roses velvety,
The air was balmy,
And the night was tender.

The table was cosy,
The food was dainty,
He was in love and she so lovely,
And the night was tender.

They sat with fingers almost touching.
They sat with eyes cast downwards.
They sat with hearts so loving,
And the night was tender.

In the muted music of the night,
In the whispers of the night,
In the secrets of the night,
And the night was tender.

Their heads were so close together,
Their lips a breath away from each other,
Yet eyes searching elsewhere,
Yet fingers reaching elsewhere .

No whispered sweet nothings,
Only the clickety-clack of keys.
No sighs of soulful longing
Only words on the screen.

They sat together with their phones,
They sat together in worlds apart.
They ate together, two solitary meals,
They spoke together, but not to each other.

This device of togetherness;
Is a voice to drive them apart.
Two souls so in touch with the world,
Two souls so lonesome in their two worlds apart.

3. NOT ROSES!

You bring me roses
From those years long ago?
You bring me the memories
Of those times lost and gone?

Why do you bring me those roses
That you had not gathered then?
Why do you make false memories
Of the moments that we never did have?

Today is all that there is,
Today is the only time I have.
My yesterday from long ago
Belongs no longer to the time that I have.

To you: I can give nothing.
Nothing remains for me to give.
Even those memories of myself;
No longer belong to me.

You give me roses from yesterday?
But where are all the thorns gone?
Bring me the thorns for I need the pain,
What are roses without the thorns?

But you bring me paper roses;
Crinkled, scentless and strong.
Where are those roses I wanted long ago,
Soft and scented, bruised and warm?

Leave those roses where they were;
Let them fade into the past.
Do not paste rough paper roses,
You cannot revisit time that was.

4. WHAT I WANT AND WHAT I NEED

What did not happen-
Maybe it was not meant to be?
I ask the question and then tell myself-
"Is this cold comfort or is this life's way?"

We never really know
Where it all went wrong.
We search for the right reason
To find why it all went wrong.

But the universe had never planned for this;
So what if I had?
Life had no place for this;
So what if I had?

I am trapped in my tiny niche,
Limited by all that's small.
I want this, I want that:
But I never know I need what.

My need the universe knows,
It is the secret that it keeps.
It is the stars that weave the pattern
Of our dreams and needs.

Why then want what is puny and closed,
When my soul can embrace the earth?
Why crave and be greedy for emptiness,
When my soul needs to be filled with the spirit of the earth?

5. IT`S MAN-FLU IF YOU PLEASE!

Sorry for my sneezes!
It's only a cold.
It's only a cold: with a geyser nose.
It's only a cold: with a razor slashed throat.
It's only a cold: with drumbeats in my head.
It's only a cold: with my wobbly legs.

Just a little cold.
I'll go and get some warm gargle.
I'll go and mop my sweat with a kitchen towel.
I'll fix me a cocktail with some pills,
I'll drink a gallon of cough syrup and some juices swill.
I'll pop in some cough drops ; that'll shut up my cough.

Of course yours isn't a silly cold: it's 'The Flu'.
Your nose is neither drippy nor leaky,
But of course that makes you cranky.
Yes, your poor voice is sore and whiny;
That's the commonest symptom
Of 'The Common Sense Allergy'.

There's the hot soup: that you couldn't swallow.
I've eaten the usual meal: I ate it 'on the go'.
I have found my blanket; I searched high and low.
You shoved your blanket off ; it's there right below.

Yes, yes! Let's just say-
That the flu has made you slow.

Of course I am vertical, mobile, bright-eyed and bushy-tailed.
Of course poor you is clingy, grouchy, grumpy and wilted.
Because- mine is only a cold; not 'The Flu'.
But yours! Yours my darling- is 'The Man Flu'.

VII. BY THE READING- LIGHT

1. THE OTHER MASK

Now the mask is worn and known,
We put it on and play by the rules.
Now the mask is worn and shown,
We put it on to prove the rules.

And yet what of that mask?
The mask that we wear beneath this one.
The mask that is sewn to the face
That stifles the real flesh and bone?

Remember that mask that you had donned all those years ago?
The mask that you had pasted on to play life's Poker game?
You had cringed without that mask to shield your open mind,
For that mask was your secure, yet living death.

Then the fates grimaced at your blank look at Life.
They were enraged at the vicious games in your Life.

They spun, wove and made a grotesque mask;
Then slapped the mask on our faces and said-
"Now 'go and face Life!'
So here you are and here I am,
Gasping in this cloth mask.
Craving the freedom to inhale,
This abundant yet forbidden breath of life.

2. THE EMBROIDERY

I took the rich silken cloth,
I had to embroider the story of my life.
I took the skeins of golden threads,
I had to sew the calendar of my days all very precise.

Each day I spent on my silk
With even stitches oh so fine.
Each hour I picked in silver and gold,
And drew the perfect pattern as planned and defined.

But then a day got a bit too busy,
Another hour got too full.
There were absurd sudden plans
And life played some peekaboo.

I hurriedly jabbed a few stitches
On a rough homespun sheet,
I poked it with some wool and needle
As I couldn't find the silk.

And so I stitched and knotted and snipped,
I toiled over that dream of mine;
Till one day I stood back and looked;
And saw that I'd only stitched together; not
embroidered at all.

With only a few skeins of silk, I'd used so much rough spun yarn.
With a few soft smooth threads, I'd used coarse wool to darn.
This was a cobbled, harum-scarum work:
A mad motley I had made, not a perfect robe.
This was not a framed and bordered tapestry of squares,
This was a lopsided, warm and absurd quilt, the living story of my years.

3. ONE DEEP BREATH

I took a deep breath,
Deep breath to inhale life.
Those shallow breaths only waft across;
They whisper and leave no ripples in their wake.
They skim over and never touch or stir,
They flit away and all remains unexplored.

I took a deep breath,
So deep that the spirit of life rushed in.
All that was jammed and clogged now burst and gushed within.
A deep breath that jerked at my being.
It hurt my ribs and pumped my heart:
It didn't matter if it was joy, or if it was the hurt.

I took a deep breath,
So deep that the essence of earth flooded me.
Sun and soil, breeze and flames poured forth from my Being.
A breath whooshed into my lungs, and energy sparkled through my veins.
It burnt my hang ups and melted my freeze,
I was tossed in a fresh flurry of illusions.

My breath has to be gusty and gutsy,
My breath has to make count every moment in life.
My breath has to be of living, and loving,
My breath has to be a storm of life.

I have to draw deeply of the stars and flowers,
I have to inhale the heat and haze.
I have to breathe in the air that's new,
I have to breathe in the hope in the dew.

I have to breathe in the courage of the night,
I have to breathe in the silence of the noon.
I have to breathe in the moon's quicksilver,
I have to breathe in the fragrance of the elements and
ether.

I took a deep breath .
I breathed in the joy of fruitful days,
I breathed in the moving breeze,
I breathed in the soul of the universe.

Then, I let out that one deep breath.
I let out all that I never needed to hold on in life.
I let out the wasted toxic fumes of hate and strife.
I took a deep, new breath: and for healing I now
made space .

4. THE WATCHER IN THE RAIN

In the silent night, the world is still and slumbering.
The darkness is a murky fog of dust and raindrops mingling.
The city lights are far and dim, the hoardings vague and blurred,
The traffic sounds are in a far off place, a muted rumbling growl.

Across the narrow cobbled street the single street light stands.
Like a grey chalk- streak of a nothingness against faceless walls.
The raindrops slither to the pavement and pool in dirty gold.
The dark night is swollen with some fear, something silent and unknown.

I stood at the window and looked into the night,
The branches crawled through the rain and reached for that street light.
That dull gleam flickered and wavered before my eyes,
What is it that stands under that street light?

Who is it that waits under that lamp, yet I cannot see him.
Who is it that waits in the rain, looking straight at me.
In that gloomy neon, he stands with no shape.

His face under that dark hood seems ancient and strange.
I peer through the foggy dark and watch the Watcher wait.
He waits with the eerie patience of an undead darkness.

For one brief moment the rain mist parts,
The streetlight pours into that pool.
I see the Watcher's eyes, opaque as the undead soul:
Dead yet burning with evil untold.

I hasten in to the familiar comfort
The world and window shut.
I clutch the phone and call a friend-
'Come help me out!'
His whisper comes over the phone-"I am on my way,
I am coming up the stairs, at long last for
I've waited from beyond the lonely grave.
I've watched and waited for you
Through rainy nights forever.
To Watch in the darkness for those that I needed to gather.
I am coming to take you out, into this rainy night.
I saw you looking into my dead eyes ,
I saw the first of your fear.
For I have been watching for you my friend
From long ago and forever.
That watch ends today my friend
Under this streetlight."

5. KINTSUGI
(Japanese art of mending broken pottery with gold lacquer)

Then the plate crashed and cracked;
No it wasn't part of a set.
It was one of those old kitchen wares
About which the cook forgets.

Someone took the broom and dustpan,
Swept aside the shards and left.
It was a lone piece, that could be whole or broken
So long as it wasn't in the way.

Then someone picked up the bits
And lay them in some order.
He wished to try his hand at a new craft,
And so put them together with gold lacquer.

The plate came together in a burst of gold;
The white was now no longer wilted or worn.
The plate now lay with a jagged shine,
It was no longer an extra, but one of a kind.

Let me 'Kintsugi' my life,
Let my brokenness heal not simply join.
Let the cracks in my life open to the light,
Let the edges boldly shine.

For what of hurts and broken bits:
Those I can bring together.
In new ways, with new thoughts,
With the strength of life's golden lacquer.

When I've healed myself with the new and pure,
My shards will softly shimmer.
My jagged edges will be filled with ragged gold,
My breaks will now be my cure.

Light will stream, and light will pour,
Through these cracks of time.
Healing balm of joy and laughter,
Will touch me with fresh new gold.

And then I'll stand, like that broken plate;
Whole and remade in all new ways.
There was nothing really lost or finished;
I was only broken out of my ordinariness.

So let me not look at the cracks of time,
Or the scarred rough ends that life often holds.
Let me gently put my broken bits together
With hope's new brush and the blessed paint of gold.

VIII. INK- SMUDGED DREAMS

1. OF MOONBEAMS AND STARDUST

Those faded old curtains:
Draw them back and let in the dark.
Gather them in folds and pin back with your chosen star.
Pluck the star from the sky above your window,
Then gather a fistful of that stardust and scatter on your pillow.

The lamp by your bedside;
Slip into its socket that yellow shiny moon.
By the glow of your reading Moon-lamp
Then read all the night through.

The night is nippy as winter has come,
So pull that fluffy cloud over, and simply snuggle down.
Cover yourself with woolly cloud
That smells of the sun and the moon.
Let yourself be cloud-hugged, and held in a happy snooze.

With sleepy eyes and wide awake imagination,
Weave a gossamer veil of dreams.
Spin the tales of shooting stars
And hear the planets sing.

Give to your life a fresh new shine
Of crazy imagination and clever fun.
Colour your soul with the quirky shades
Of life's broken and stubby crayons.

2. COME STAND BY THE OCEAN

There is an ocean that is in the horizon,
An ocean that lies beyond our time.
It surges with the waves of all that is and will be,
It laps on the shores with the foam of all that has been.

That is the ocean that belongs to today, as well as the days of yore.
An ocean that swells with the here and the now,
Then recedes with the murmurs of long ago.
I will stand on its great shore
And listen to its mighty roar.
I will play in the surf and flail in the waves,
For therein nothing matters anymore.

That ocean is there for all our times, and the many lives to come.
It washes away all our years and cleanses all our deeds.
It rushes forth with relentless power and covers the sands of time,
It gurgles back beyond our reach and leaves forgotten stories on the beach.

By this ocean I will stand
And watch the endless waves.

The waves will roar with my angers
And mourn with all my pains.

Then these towering waves will rise to new heights.
They will rise; come what may, for it matters not what was yearned.
It matters not what was gained , it matters not why I failed.
It matters not why it pained, it matters not, whence the pain.

This is the ocean beyond time,
The ocean of eternity.
Nothing counts here: not you nor me or even us,
We are the pebbles washed out by the sea.

By this ocean of the ages
We can imagine what might have been.
We can tell the tales of the past
Or talk some more of all that could have been.

Nothing matters not hearts nor hours,
There is just the whisper of the waves.
They come to go, and go to come,
Nothing is lost and nothing is gained.

Come! In this ocean we will gently wet our weary feet.
These waters that flow over us

Will wash the dust off our deeds.
In this ocean we will touch, the waters of eternity.

If we did not meet our dreams in life
It was never meant to be.
Come by the ocean and watch the waves
Toss and retrieve all those dreams.

3. RAINY TWILIGHT

The twilight melted into a silver grey,
The dying light was fused in the rain.
A sudden shower caught the day of March
In a surprise flurry of rain.

The sidewalk glinted with puddles of neon,
The cars a blend of mud and chrome,
The street lights were bathed in that spray,
The wet shadows flowed into the day.

City lights, lamp lights, shop lights, home lights:
Lights that mellowed in the rain.
The dry leaves swirled in the gust,
And the branches drank in the rain.

People slowed and gasped with delight;
Faces upturned to taste the rain.
Fingers stretched and eyes closed;
To touch, feel and hold the rain.

In the midst of heated hurry,
In the midst of determined haste,
A restful pause, a fleeting taste,
A wash of freshness in the soft summer rain.

Just a respite, just a promise,
A gentle word from heaven to say:
'Day is done; may you find heart's ease,
And give thanks for all your life's days'.

4. NIGHT SKY

Night sky!
City lights gleam in the distant dark
While star light spills on the dinghy car park.

Night sky!
The horizon is diffused with a neon glow,
The street lights stand in strict row but with a halo of dull gold.

Night sky!
The roads are restless with the blinding headlights,
Those hoardings dazzle and shimmer with winking party lights.

Night sky!
The apartments look so cosy with bits and slivers of lights,
Somewhere glows a loud TV screen, and somewhere a drowsy night light.

Night sky!
Up there above be me twinkle a myriad stars.
The clouds are pearly with moonlight, and silvery with starlight.

Night sky!

That starlight seems so close up and familiar at the end of the day.

All the glitzy party lights are far off, but the stardust is just for me.

5. THE HERE AND THE NOW

Leave it all behind and just go!
Let go and turn the corner.
Say goodbye to yesterday,
Move on, walk away!

Drop the baggage, lose the weights,
Stow the worries and bury the thoughts.
Sweep the mess and clear the clutter,
Move on, walk away!

Start afresh, make new beginnings.
Reach for that which has always been out of reach.
Call out to the future and draw it closer,
Welcome that voice you had heard from afar.

Yet there will be that moment and the hour;
When you will stop and turn.
You will look back and think of all that was,
And you will wish to go back.

For this freshness is not the new you sought,
This beginning is not your start.
This day is not a new day;
For you miss those days of the past.

Tell yourself: nothing gets left, nothing gets lost,
The new is always a part of the old.
Hearts do not forget and freedom never denies
What life has given to what life offers henceforth.

Do not wish away what is there,
Or mourn for what might have been.
What was meant to be will always be:
A promise made, a promise kept, by life, to you and me.

6. FIND YOUR MAGIC

Magic trails and lingers in all the corners of the lanes.
Magic drifts across all of life's busy mains.
Magic swirls in the smoke of the stove.
Magic curls in the puff of the clouds.

Magic surrounds my humble home,
Magic enters with the key at the door.
Magic twirls to the radio song,
Magic bubbles in the soup in the pan.

Look for magic; because magic is there.
Look for magic in that which you see and hear.
Look for magic in that dusty urn;
Magic will surprise you with flowers unknown.

Open the old door that you never went to;
Magic will lead you to the secret garden just through.
Open a well loved book of the olden days,
Magic will fly you to forbidden places.

Make magic when the sky is grey:
With broken crayons from a dusty shelf.
Make magic when the day is dull, and the mood is low,
See how your dress catches the rainbow.

Go out to find magic at every turn and nook.
Taste the magic at the ice cream booth.
Go out and toss the ordinary beans;
Then climb the stalk to capture some moonbeams.

Lose that slipper, follow the White Rabbit.
Find the Prince, and have a tea party.
Hold the rose and bite the apple.
Find the Beast and outwit evil.

The brooms and the wings, the halos and the hands;
Magic has its marvel wands.
A little chuckle, a tiny pat:
That's the secret magic chant.

Magic is in the wind and the sea.
Magic is there in you and me.
Open your heart: let magic flow,
Imagine, and let your magic glow.

www.ingramcontent.com/pod-product-compliance
Ingram Content Group UK Ltd.
Pitfield, Milton Keynes, MK11 3LW, UK
UKHW041957190726
13854UKWH00005B/2032

9 789354 270284